Alfred's Basic Piano Library
Piano

Fun Book · Level 1B

A COLLECTION OF 24 ENTERTAINING SOLOS

FUN BOOK 1B of Alfred's Basic Piano Library contains 24 short pieces, carefully coordinated PAGE BY PAGE with the material in LESSON BOOK 1B. These pieces serve to make the course more flexible and more easily adaptable to the taste and needs of the individual student. They may be used *in addition to* or *instead of* the pieces in RECITAL BOOK 1B, to provide additional reinforcement to the concepts each piece contains as well as extra reading material at the proper level of advancement.

This book also answers the often expressed need for a variety of supplementary material for use when two or more students from the same family are studying from the same course and prefer not to play exactly the same pieces.

There is no substitute for good humor at the piano lesson, and a smiling student is obviously a happy student. The subjects for the selections composed especially for this book have been suggested by students and teachers, and it is our hope that this book will be found to live up to its name, for teachers as well as for students.

The Authors

 A General MIDI disk is available (8586) which includes a full piano recording and background accompaniment.

Will You, Won't You?

Use after MONEY CAN'T BUY EV'RYTHING!
LESSON BOOK 1B (page 8).

Adapted from "Alice in Wonderland."
by Lewis Carroll

Moderately fast

mf "Walk a lit-tle fast-er," said the tor-toise to the snail, "There's a

por-poise close be- hind me, and he's tread-ing on my tail!"

A little faster, very rhythmically

f Will you, won't you, will you, won't you, will you join the dance?

Will you, won't you, will you, won't you, Won't you join the dance?

Surprise!

Use after GRANDPA'S CLOCK (page 10).

Happily

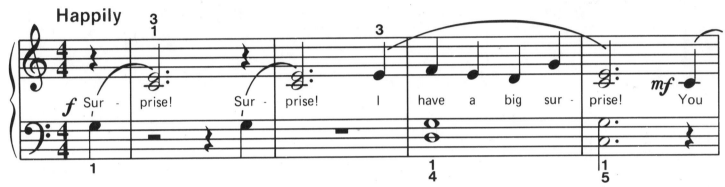

f Sur - prise! Sur - prise! I have a big sur - prise! *mf* You

need - n't hold your hands out, You need - n't close your eyes. *f* Sur - prise! Sur -

prise! This won't take ver - y long; *mf* The big sur - prise is sim - ply this:

slowing - -

faster

Both hands one octave lower - - - - - -

f I've learned to play this song! *(Spoken)* Sur - prise!

4

Knock, Knock!

Use after WHEN THE SAINTS GO MARCHING IN (page 11).

Moderately fast

If you'd like to play this game again, here's more:

Knock, knock! Who's there?
Boo—! Boo— who?
Didn't mean to make you cry!
That's an awful joke. Ha-ha!

Knock, knock! Who's there?
Wanda! Wanda who?
"Wanda where the money goes!"
That's an awful joke. Ha-ha!

Use after JOIN THE FUN (page 13).

Old Woman

Folk song

Moderately fast

Old wo - man, old wo - man, would you like to wash my shirts?

Speak a lit - tle loud - er sir, I'm ver - y hard of hear - ing.

Old wo - man, old wo - man, would you like to mar - ry me?

Law's a mer - cy, hal - le - lu - jah, now I hear you clear - ly!

6

Für Ludwig*

Use after THE CLOWN (page 15).

Not too fast, but with great optimism

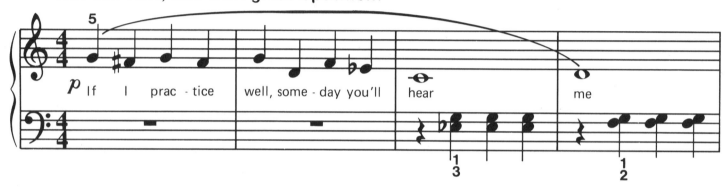

p If I prac - tice | well, some - day you'll | hear | me

Play Beet - ho - ven's | mu - sic with great | ease.

mf If I prac - tice | well, some - day you'll | hear | me

Play that mu - sic | he wrote for E - | lise.

One octave lower

*Ludwig van Beethoven—Composer of *Für Elise* (For Elise).

Use after GOOD KING WENCESLAS (page 18).

A Prayer for Peace

MIDDLE C POSITION

Andante moderato

1. Let us say a prayer for peace all a-round the world.
2. Let us pray that strife will cease all a-round the world.

Come and join us in our prayer for all peo-ple ev-'ry-where,

"Fa-ther keep us in Thy care, all a-round the world!"

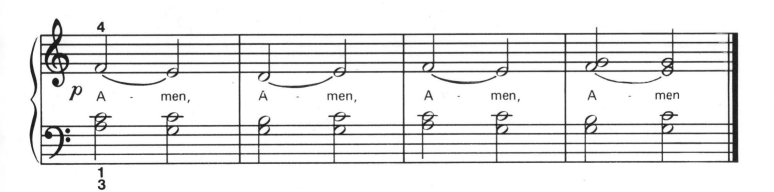

A - men, A - men, A - men, A - men

The Purple Cow

Use after THE RAINBOW (page 19).

Words by Gelett Burgess

Allegro moderato

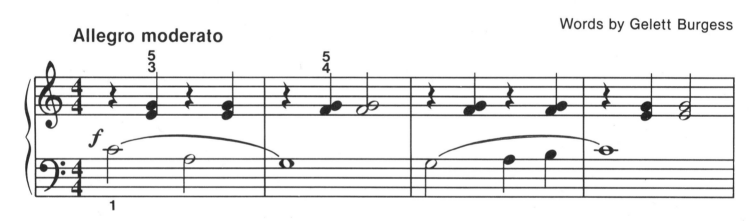

never saw a pur-ple cow, I nev-er hope to see one, But

gradually slower to 𝄐

I can tell you an-y-how, I'd rath-er see than be one!

resume original tempo

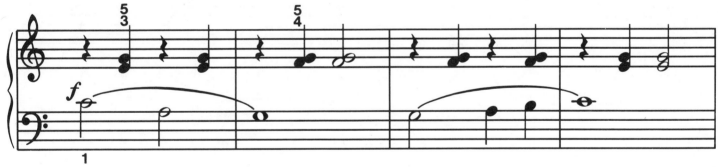

gradually slower to end

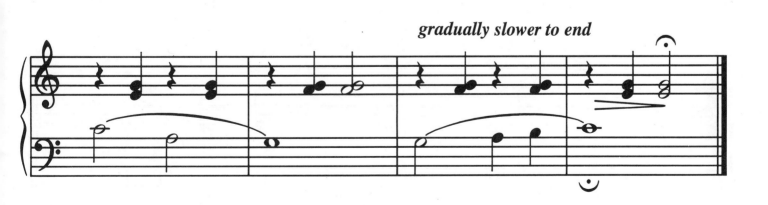

Whoopee Ti-Yi-Yo

Use after HAPPY BIRTHDAY TO YOU! (page 21).

Cowboy song

Allegro moderato

Whoop-ee ti - yi - yo, Get a - long, lit - tle do - gies, It's

your mis - for - tune and none of my own; Whoop - ee

ti - yi - yo, Get a - long, lit - tle do - gies, For you

know Wy - om - ing will be your new home!

*A "dogie" is an orphaned calf. The first syllable, "do," rhymes with "go."

Use after INDIANS (page 24).

Barrel of Monkeys!

G POSITION

12

Amigos

Use after NEW G POSITION (page 25).

Brightly

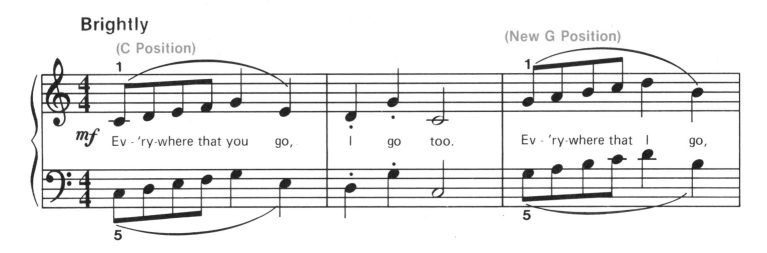

(C Position)

mf Ev - 'ry-where that you go, I go too.

(New G Position)

Ev - 'ry-where that I go,

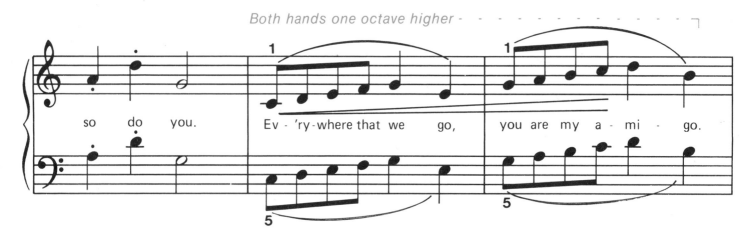

so do you.

Both hands one octave higher - - - - - - - - - - - -

Ev - 'ry-where that we go, you are my a - mi - go.

Both hands one octave lower - - - - - - - - - - - -

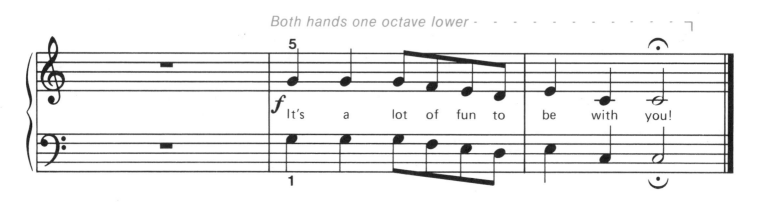

f It's a lot of fun to be with you!

Who Did?

Use after HARP SONG (page 27) or CONCERT TIME (page 28).

NEW G POSITION

Brightly

f Who did? Who did? Who did? Who did? Who did swal - low Jo - nah?

Both hands one octave lower -

p Who did? Who did? Who did? Who did? Who did swal - low Jo - nah?

Whale did swal - low Jo - nah, Whale did swal - low Jo - nah,

(Both hands as written)

Whale did swal - low Jo - nah down!

If you'd like to play it twice, here's another verse:

Who did? Who did? Who did? Who did?
Who found little Moses? *(etc.)*

Pharaoh's daughter found him, Found him in the water
Pharaoh's daughter found him there!

Can't Get 'Em Up!

Use after A COWBOY'S SONG (page 30).

Military bugle call

Allegro

f We can't get 'em up, we can't get 'em up, we can't get 'em up this morn - ing! We

can't get 'em up, we can't get 'em up, we can't get 'em up to - day!

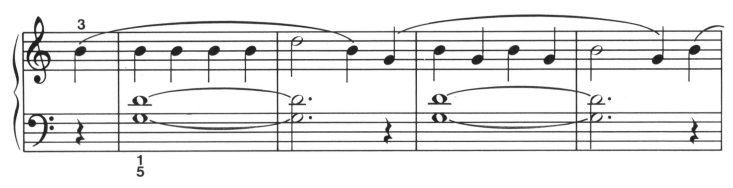

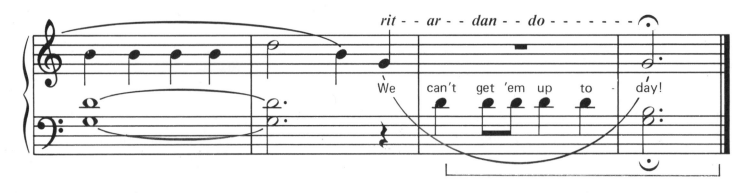

rit - - ar - - dan - - do - - - - - - -

We can't get 'em up to - day!

Use after THE MAGIC MAN (page 32).

Music with a Beat

Rock tempo

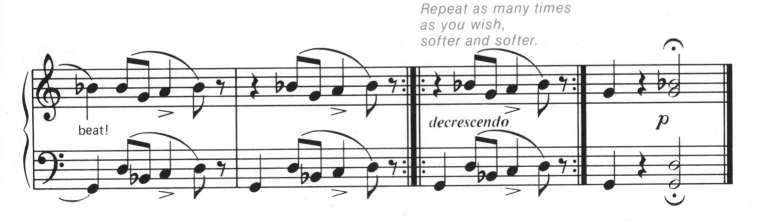

Boogie-Woogie Goose

Use after THE MAGIC MAN (page 32).

Allegro moderato

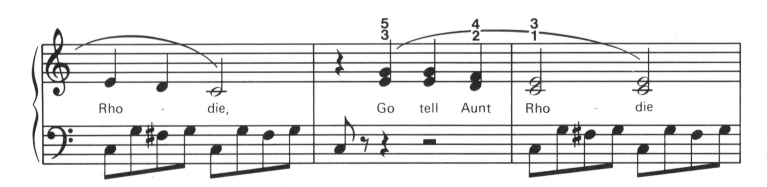

*Pairs of eighth notes may be played a bit unevenly, in a "lilting" style:

long   short, long   short, etc.

Ain't Gonna Rain

Use after THE GREATEST SHOW ON EARTH (page 34).

MIDDLE D POSITION

Allegro moderato

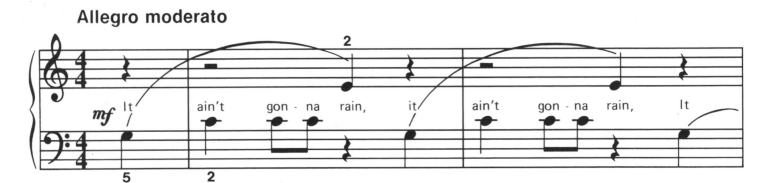

mf It ain't gon - na rain, it ain't gon - na rain, It

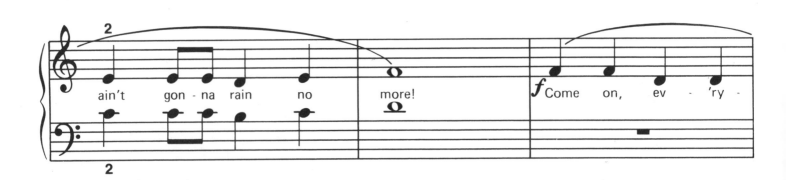

ain't gon - na rain no more! *f* Come on, ev - 'ry -

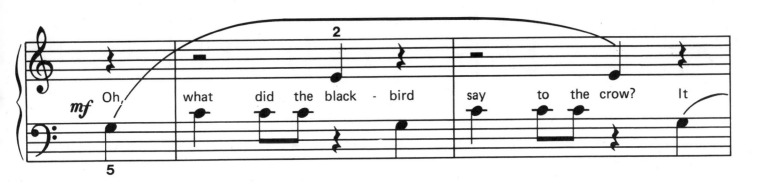

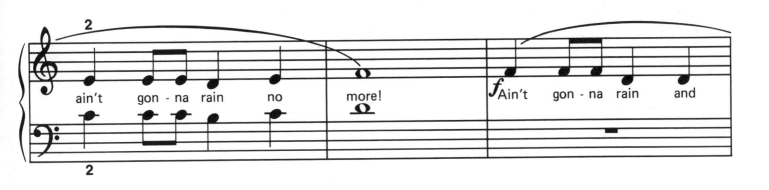

Use after THE GREATEST SHOW ON EARTH (page 34).

Happy Day Polka

MIDDLE D POSITION

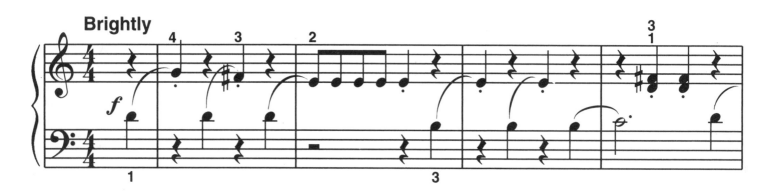

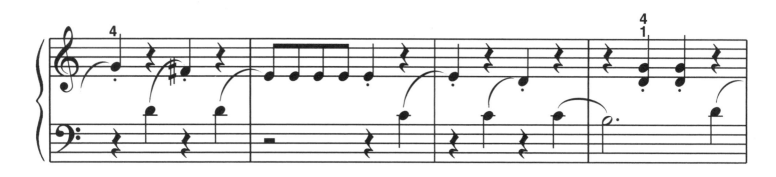

Fine

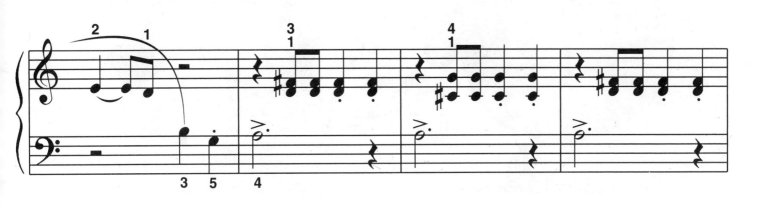

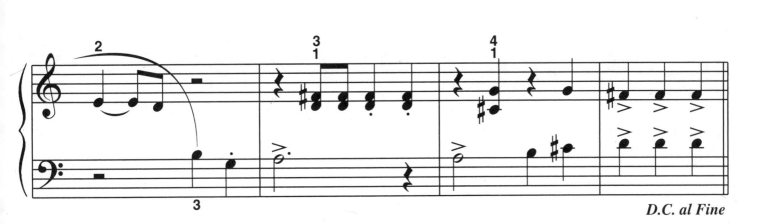

D.C. al Fine

On With the Show!

Use after MEASURING HALF-STEPS (page 36).

March tempo

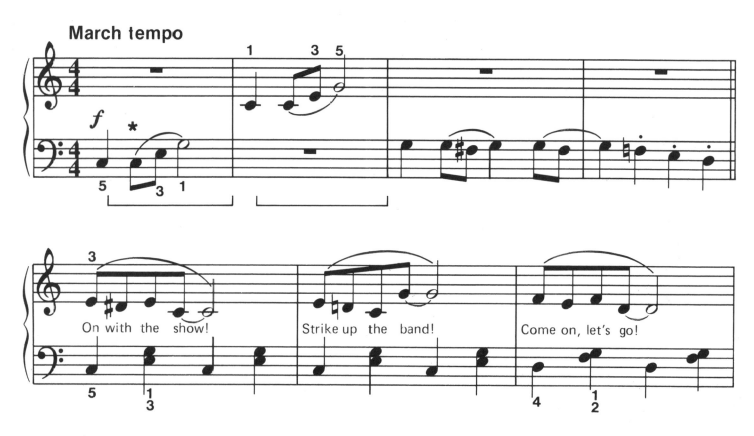

On with the show! Strike up the band! Come on, let's go!

*Pairs of eighth notes may be played a bit unevenly, in a "lilting" style:

long short, long short, etc.

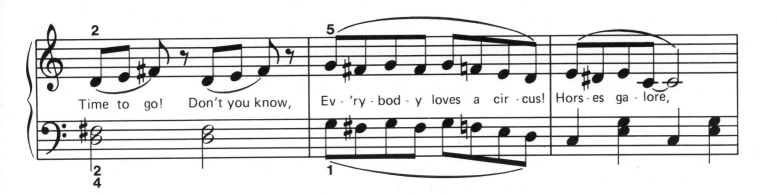

The Howling Wind

Use after THE WHIRLWIND (page 37).

MIDDLE D "HALF-STEP" POSITION

Mysteriously

When at night it's rain-ing, and the wind is blow-ing strong;

Howl-ing 'round my win-dow with a sad and mourn-ful song,

I'm not real-ly fright-tened when I cov-er up my head;

I'm just glad I'm snug-gled in my bed!

God Made Them All

Use after THE PLANETS (page 39).

Three Wise Monkeys

Use after THE KEY OF G MAJOR (page 42).

KEY OF G MAJOR
Key Signature: one sharp (F♯)

HAND POSITION: L.H. plays lower tetrachord,
R.H. plays upper tetrachord.

Allegro moderato

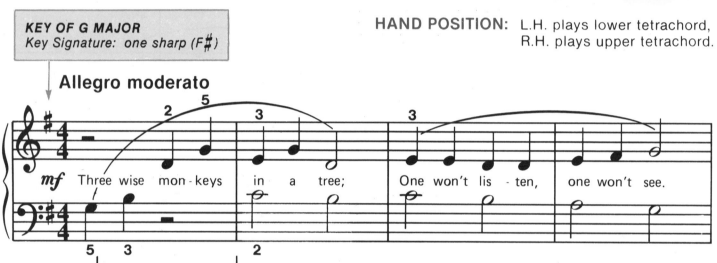

Three wise mon-keys in a tree; One won't lis-ten, one won't see.

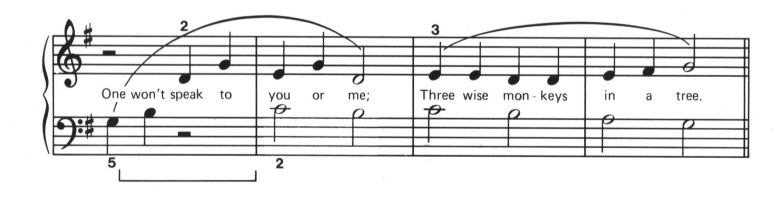

One won't speak to you or me; Three wise mon-keys in a tree.

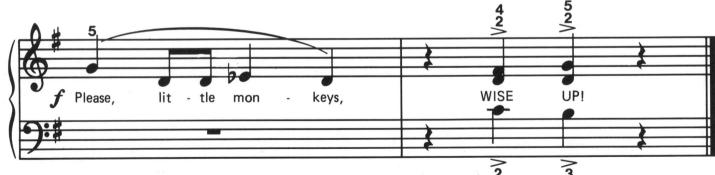

Please, lit-tle mon-keys, WISE UP!

FOR MORE FUN: **Play also in C TETRACHORD POSITION (5's on C's one octave apart).**

The Brave Knight

Use after THE KEY OF G MAJOR (page 42).

HAND POSITION: L.H. plays lower tetrachord,
R.H. plays upper tetrachord.

KEY OF G MAJOR
Key Signature: one sharp (F♯)

FOR MORE FUN: Play also in C TETRACHORD POSITION (5's on C's one octave apart).

The Baseball Game

Use after FRENCH LULLABY (page 43).

R.H. in C POSITION
L.H. in LOW G POSITION

March tempo

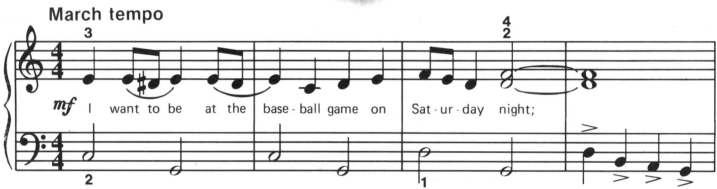

I want to be at the base-ball game on Sat-ur-day night;

I want to see that we win that game on Sat-ur-day night!

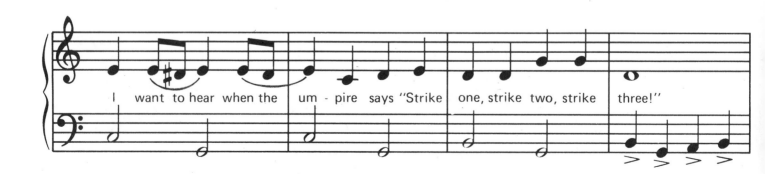

I want to hear when the um-pire says "Strike one, strike two, strike three!"

I want to see ev-'ry-thing there is to see! And when our
team comes to bat I will jump and yell and hol-ler and call,
f And when they swing I will sing, "Sock that ball o-ver the wall!"
Watch-ing a game is a lot of fun when our play-ers knock out a big home run, and
rit - - ar - - dan - - do
I want to be there to see them hit that ball!
Play ball!

Use after SONATINA (page 44).

The Future Belongs to the Young

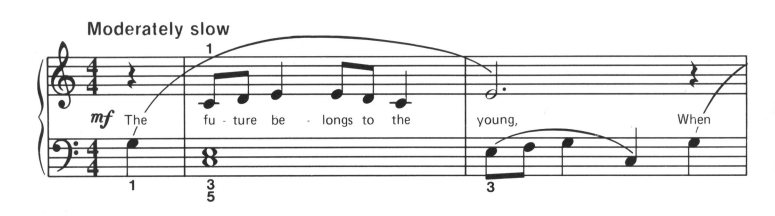

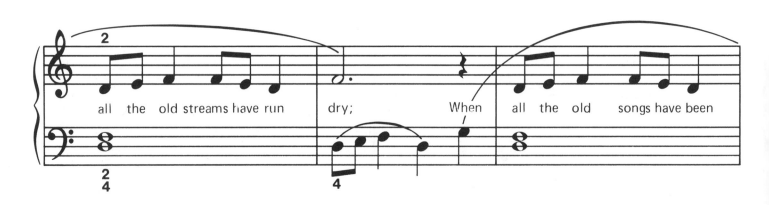

sung,   When   all the old dreams are gone   by.   When

all the old pa - ges are   turned,   When   all the old   bells have been

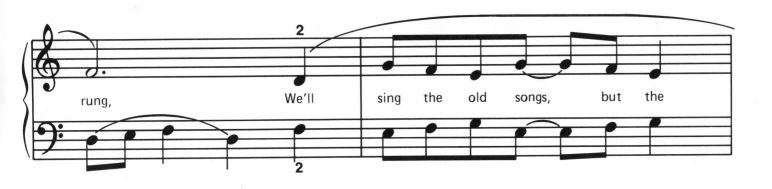

rung,   We'll   sing the old songs,   but the

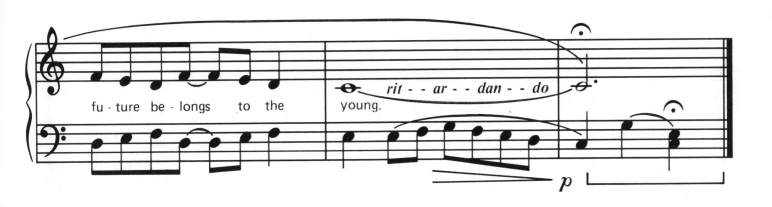

fu - ture be - longs   to the   young.   *rit - - ar - - dan - - do*

Ta-dah!

Use after SONATINA (page 44).

R.H. in C POSITION
L.H. in G POSITION

Allegro

Both hands one octave higher

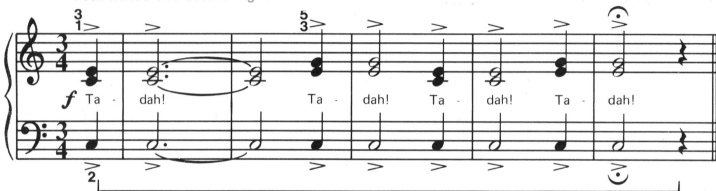

f Ta - dah! Ta - dah! Ta - dah! Ta - dah!

**With great pomp and power,
Not too slow!**

(R.H. as written)

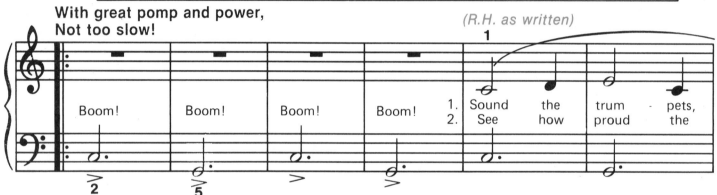

Boom! Boom! Boom! Boom!
1. Sound the trum - pets,
2. See how proud the

L.H. one octave lower

here I come! Ring the bells and rat - tle the drum!
peo - ple look! Shake my hand, I fin - ished the book!

Both hands one octave higher

rit - - ar - - dan - - do

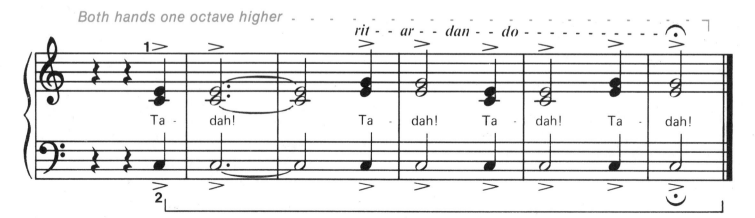

Ta - dah! Ta - dah! Ta - dah! Ta - dah!